For Kit Holme

First published in 2024

Text copyright © Kathryn Holme 2024
Illustrations copyright © Maggie Bolton 2024

ISBN 978-1-7384569-0-1

Published by Untitled 64 publishing

UNTITLED
64

Captain Kit

Written by
Kathryn Holme

Illustrated by
Maggie Bolton

Captain Kit was a pirate
who sailed the seven seas.
He wore a stripy T-shirt and
shorts down to his knees.

His big hat matched his boots,
they were all a shiny black.
His sword was made of chocolate
in case he needed a snack.

**His ship was called the Yum Yum-
it was full of tasty treats.**

**Captain Kit loved snacking.
He would eat and eat and eat!**

WANTED

cake

sweets

Yo ho ho for Captain Kit
aboard his ship, the Yum Yum.

See him eating everything,
filling up his tum tum.

Shipmates Joy and Pedro tried to hide the food one day.

Captain Kit just sniffed the air and found it straightaway.

"Now what shall we do?"
cried Joy.
"We need a plan, I think.

If Captain Kit keeps
eating, the Yum Yum's
bound to sink."

"You're quite right," agreed Pedro. "Let's wait till he's asleep.

Then throw the food overboard into the sea so deep."

Yo ho ho for Captain Kit
aboard his ship, the Yum Yum.

See him eating everything,
filling up his tum tum.

While Captain Kit was sleeping,
they grabbed the cakes and buns.

They fired them all into the sea
from cannons and musket guns.

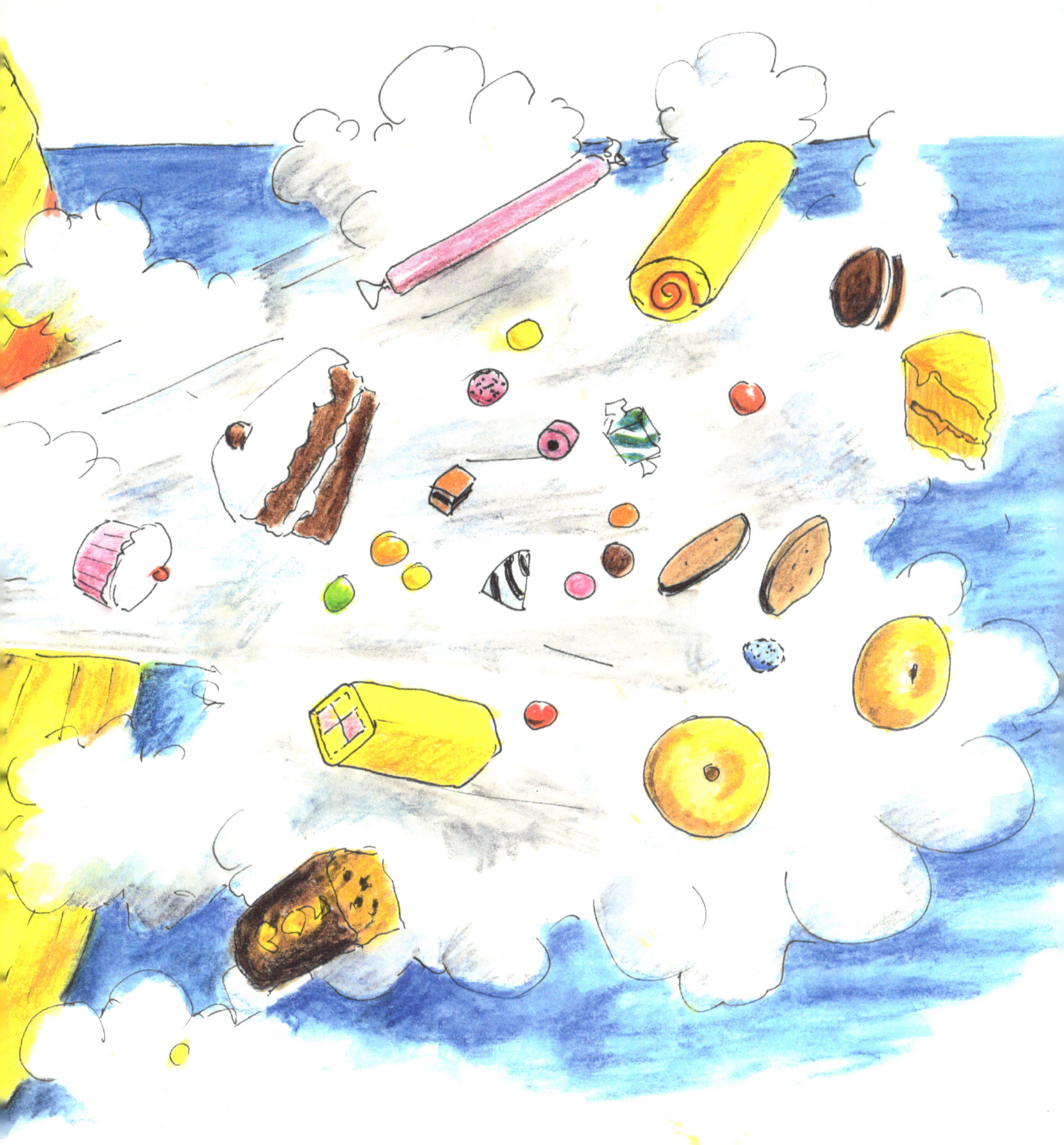

Then they heard a scary roar.
Joy and Pedro gasped in fright.

As from the ocean's waves,
a monster came into sight.

It was huge, red and scaly
and in an angry mood.

"How dare you throw
cakes at me.
What a shocking
waste of food."

Yo ho ho for Captain Kit
aboard his ship, the Yum Yum.

See him eating everything,
filling up his tum tum.

Captain Kit was now awake
and surprised by what he saw.

A monster eating all his treats,
stuffing them in its jaws.

"Stop!" he cried.
"Those are my cakes."
But the monster didn't care.

So, Captain Kit said nicely,
"Come aboard and
we can share."

"Oh no," said Pedro sadly.

"A disaster!" Joy agreed.
"It's clear our plan didn't work
as we've now got two to feed."

Yo ho ho for Captain Kit aboard his ship, the Yum Yum.

See him eating everything, filling up his tum tum.

The monster climbed onto the deck,
it brought a recipe book.

"If you let me join your crew,
I will teach you how to cook."

**It made them lots of salads
and healthy plant-based eats.
And many tasty types of
low-fat, low-sugar treats.**

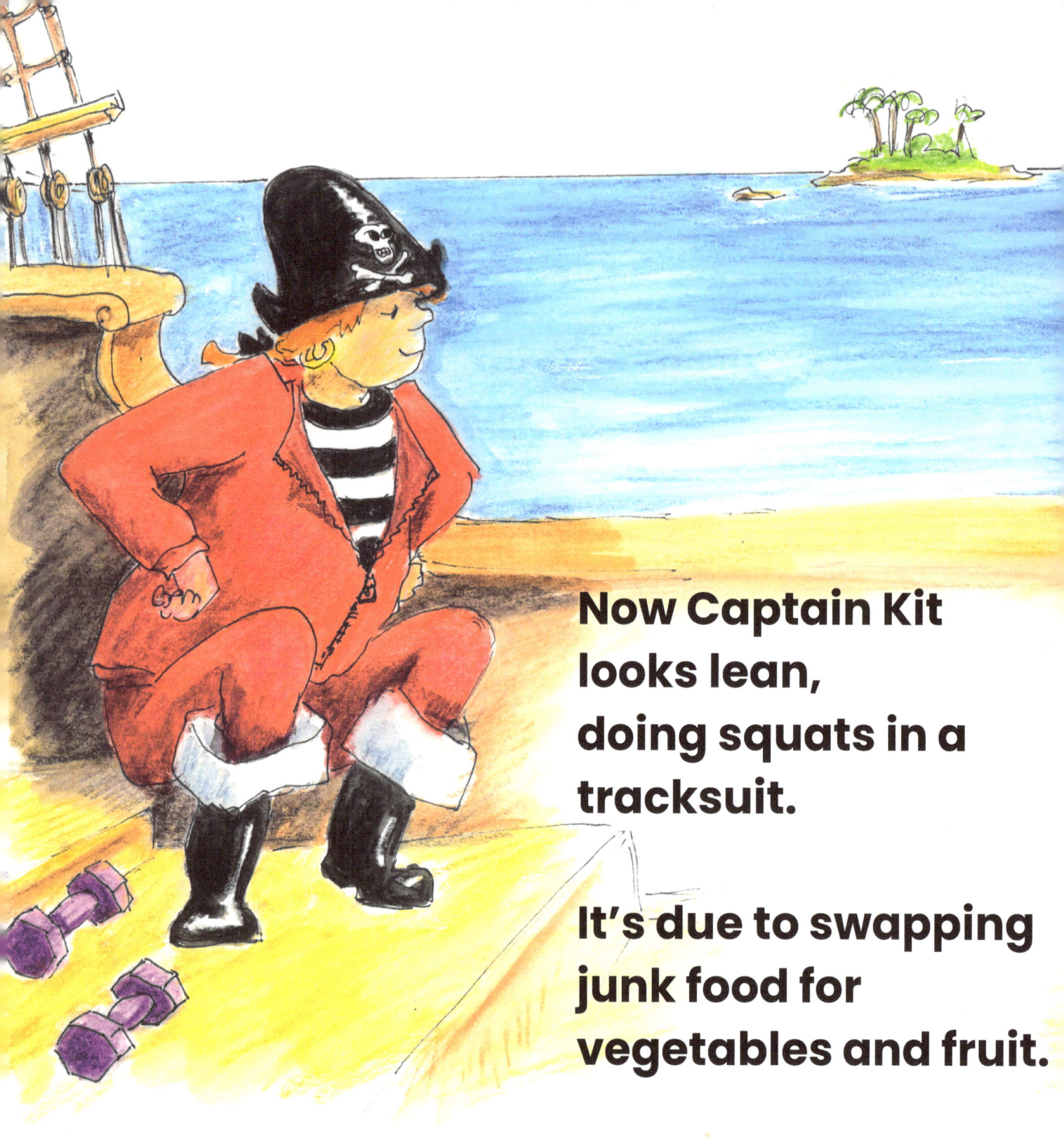

Now Captain Kit
looks lean,
doing squats in a
tracksuit.

It's due to swapping
junk food for
vegetables and fruit.

Yo ho ho for Captain Kit aboard his ship, the Yum Yum.

See him eating healthily and admire his toned tum.

Milton Keynes UK
Ingram Content Group UK Ltd.
UKHW052153030924
447804UK00002B/18